JOURNEY TO WHOLENESS

Healing the Past,
Embracing Change,
and Learning to Let Go

SARAH MOON

Journey to Wholeness:
Healing the Past, Embracing Change, and Learning to Let Go

MOON, SARAH, Author
JOURNEY TO WHOLENESS
SARAH MOON

ISBN: 979-8-9878407-1-9 (eBook)
ISBN: 979-8-9878407-0-2 (Paperback)
ISBN: 979-8-9878407-2-6 (Audiobook)

Book Interior and E-book Design by Amit Dey | amitdey2528@gmail.com
Recording of the book: Blue Form Media | blueformmedia@gmail.com

SEL042000
SEL023000

QUANTITY PURCHASES: Schools, companies, professional groups, clubs, and other organizations may qualify for special terms when ordering quantities of this title.

For information visit totalityworkshop.com

INTRODUCTION

Life can be overwhelming, scary, sad, lonely, unfair, undesirable, unhealthy, scarce of abundance, dark, all kinds of low vibration and intimidating. However, we can turn things around! Our minds create the life we live.

I believe we are eternal; we are on a journey back to God. We are individual souls, all helping each other find our way home. We are walking the journey, one step at a time. This book is made of things that I've learned along the way. Some are simple and as plain as the nose on my face… I had to discover and search for others. I truly hope you'll enjoy the read! I've enjoyed writing, sharing and applying what I've learned. This book is full of hope! Hope that it can be of help to you, the reader.

Quick disclaimer, I believe in God. As you read this book, feel free to replace the word 'God' with whatever you believe in. Everything in this book is my opinion/way to look at life. This book is a condensed summary of some of the things I've learned on my journey to wholeness.

Make today a fabulous day!

TABLE OF CONTENTS

1. WORDS ARE POWERFUL

A little over a decade ago, I used to go to the gym, workout and go to the sauna. There was an oriental couple who would go to the sauna at the same time as me. They spoke broken English and we always made small talk. One evening, the guy sat by me bumping me with enough force to make me move. He got my full attention. Then with his index finger he made a circle in the air in front of his face, he said very loudly, "Why you happy? You always happy! Life is not that good!"

After I got over the shock of being bumped, I sat there and smiled. You see, I had been working hard at changing my words in thought and in speech to being positive and kind. It worked! It showed up on the outside! I told him that I changed my thinking and speech to make life that good. Our thoughts are made of words. The words we focus on, repeat constantly in the silence of our thoughts or the ones we speak out loud - those words produce the life we live. The doubts. and fears are very powerful! Negative words/thoughts are more influential than positive ones, and we tend to fear more than trust…all the time. In the quiet of our minds, we question our decisions, we doubt the outcome and fear failure. We may never pronounce those words, but they will appear if we keep on creating whatever it is in our minds. I love this beautiful quote, it says it perfectly:

"There is freedom waiting for you,
On the breezes of the sky,
And you ask "What if I fall?"
Oh but my darling, What if
you fly?"

—Erin Hanson

When we were born, we were free, happy and our light shone brightly! Have you looked into a baby's eyes lately? What did you see? There is love, tenderness, power, absolutely no doubt!

The scriptures invite us to be as little children… where have we changed? Where have we given up? I have given power to people in my life to influence how I feel about myself. Their words and actions had the power to make me feel great with a compliment and awful with a criticism. So sad!

By the way, there is no such a thing as constructive criticism. Either you build someone up or you tear them down. You can't do both at the same time. Our families are the worst! Because we love them, we get "hurt" by their "words" and deeds. "Word" is powerful - that's how God created the world, you and me! Listen carefully and speak kindly.

I AM are the two most powerful words on the planet! Whatever we put behind it, sticks! So, BE CAREFUL with the "I AM…" statements!!!

- I am dumb/stupid. You might have done something dumb/stupid.
  It does not make you dumb/stupid. What do I mean? Replace it with "That was dumb/stupid, not doing it again."

- I am broke, I can't afford it. Not really. If money is tight, it still doesn't "break" you. But if you keep saying it, you will keep feeling like it and seeing it in your life. How does this sound?
"Finances have been challenging, I am open to/ creating new financial solutions for myself."

- I am sick. I hear that when people have a little sniffle. How can you change that? "I am feeling better," "I am getting better," "I am getting healthier." Even when you are very ill, don't own the disease so it doesn't own you!

You see, the brain is amazing and very trusting of you. Yup! That is right! Your voice (vocal or thought) is what the brain trusts. We create what we think and say. So, be mindful of your focus! Focus on good/high vibration emotions/ light/loving/ merciful/ judgment free WORDS! Words that make you feel good and smile.

Listen to understand, people will open up when they feel safe. Some people open up even when it is not safe and get hurt because of it. Be the safe harbor and don't judge or gossip about it. The world has enough judgment and falsehoods out there. Speak kindly to and about people, self included.

We have no idea what their journey feels like to them and the choices they made along the way. Don't take things personal. Keep in mind:

> "People's opinion of me is none of my business."

It really isn't. It is all about them: how they are feeling at that moment and how they see life, people, events. Sometimes, people are hurting so bad that they feel the need to hurt someone else, and most of the time, it is the ones they love most that get the brunt of it. This is unfortunate, but real. DON'T TAKE IT PERSONAL! IT IS NOT ABOUT YOU.

Speak kindly to them and to yourself. Avoid saying:

- I hate myself.
- I am so lonely.
- I am broken.
- I don't know what to do, I give up.
- I am powerless,
- What's the use?
- Life sucks.

How about changing it up a bit?

- I love myself, I love you. (If that is too hard, how about I am working on loving myself, I like you)
- I am surrounded by people, I am reaching out, I am connecting.
- I've been broken, I am putting myself back together again, one piece at a time.
- I am searching for solutions, I am listening for answers.
- I am empowered by God, I am able to do all things through Him.

- This trial is coming through and I am better for it, keeping the lessons.
- Life has ups and downs, climbing out of this down.
- Lessons can be hard, I am better for it.

We BELIEVE, CREATE AND LIVE the words we think and speak every single day. Speak empowering words in your mind, heart and with your voice. Create a "meter" that measures the emotions evoked by your words. If they are of low vibration/dark/negative, and make you feel less than the beautiful soul that God created in you, don't waste anymore time focusing on them. DELETE and REPLACE them!

Speak kind/loving words into your existence. Vibrate them into life and watch God work through you to help His children find hope, joy, happiness and wholeness in life and in themselves.

Words also may shatter hearts, create doubt, fear resentment, bitterness, hopelessness, hatred, sadness and all bad things. Sometimes I turn off my "word meter" and allow myself a few hours of misery because I get tired of it all. I used to not have a "meter," which was very painful. Now, it may be a 1/2 day of misery, then I realize how bad/yucky it feels and put my meter on max.

When someone speaks or writes hurtful words to you, ask the person if that is what they mean. Don't "ASS-U-ME" anything. Communication can be very flawed at times, and misunderstandings happen more often than not.

Speak your truths with kindness.

This way, the Spirit of God can do the testifying for you. Listen to people without internalizing the words, so people have no power on how you feel about yourself and life. LET IT GO!!! Words create life! Make it beautiful!

SMALL CHECK UP:

1. Would I like to be spoken to the way I speak to people?

2. Am I speaking my truths with kindness, so I can keep my dignity and the person listening can keep theirs?

3. Am I internalizing words that are spoken to me? Do I still have the power to decide how I feel about myself and life? Have I given power away?

4. Do I get offended/hurt easily? Do I over-think things?

5. Are my words positive, empowering and light?

6. Am I communicating or just speaking? Am I being understood? Am I understanding people?

7. Am I patrolling my thoughts? Are the words I am thinking kind towards myself and others?

2. TAKE ACTION

We usually RE-act instead of taking a moment to think/process and take action to move things forward in a better way. RE-action has the tendency of speaking out of negative emotions (hurt, anger, judgment, fear, inadequacy, frustration, hatred, etc.) and feeds the fire, making it bigger, hotter and worse.

We are created to ACT, create, love, be loved, achieve, learn, teach, be abundant, share, care: all the things of goodness and light. There is opposition in all things. That has a purpose: it is to entice men and women one way or the other. So we may choose by exercising agency. Agency is the only thing that is truly ours. Our own bodies are not ours to command. It breathes on its own, it digests whatever we put into it, the heart beats without us having to think about it. Think about the miracle that we are and think of how much we do not do for ourselves: it just is. However, through our agency, we choose to act or RE-act, act or be ACTED upon.

I was part of an argument and the other person kept on saying things that were belittling and if allowed to be, they were downright hurtful. However, instead of belittling back, I listened to understand where they were coming from. I know that those who speak hurtful things are hurting the most, so, I did listen with the intent to understand, not reply, defend/attack...I was able to speak my truths with kindness, no anger in my words and we both kept our dignity intact when I spoke. The beauty of this is, one cannot argue with truth and kindness.

How do you choose? "Shoot - aim" or "look - see - aim - shoot"? What do I mean by that? Have you ever said something hurtful to someone that had said something hurtful to you simply out of reflex? I know I have. It takes seconds to produce many hours/days/months/sometimes years of hurt that need to be repaired.

Taking action requires living in your own power, being comfortable in your own skin, speaking from the heart and listening to understand - not quickly reply out of self defense. Taking action requires self-mastery. It also requires tough skin. Nothing has the power to offend your soul because you are a person of action. Sometimes action is silence. We don't need to reply to every conversation or be a part of every argument to which we are invited. Yikes! "But it is personal!" Nope, it is not. It is not about you, it is about how they are feeling at that moment.

By the same token, self-mastery doesn't speak hurtful/fighting words to self or others. Gossipers don't need us to respond or defend. Critics don't need us to justify ourselves from their opinion. Time will tell the truth. Judgmental people don't need our time. You read it right: they are going to judge regardless, whether or not we listen or reply to it. That's on them, not us.

Manipulators have no power if we stand our ground and do what we think needs done. The end. Narcissists are smart and very deceiving. Again, self-mastery will keep them far, far away as we become too powerful, too independent for them to look at us as their next victim. Last but not least, fearful/doubtful people are highly contagious. We have the power to either let them connect to us in fear/doubt - RE-action - or, we have the power to keep them away, walking in faith and expecting miracles.

Sometimes, okay, a lot of times, we RE-act without thinking. Self defense would be the operative solution. However, when we speak in fear, anger, hurt, frustration, rage, doubt... we are not speaking our truths. It would be wise to listen to our hearts and see what emotion is ruling at the moment. If it is not an emotion of light and high vibration, don't open your mouth! And delete the thought!

Remember: people will say and do whatever they do because of how they are feeling inside. It is not about you! Take NOTHING personal. That should take the spring right out from under the RE-act button, taking away its power.

To the people we love the most, we give all the power that triggers us. They are our loved ones and should "know us best, they should care for our feelings and love us." Again, stop RE-acting in the heat of the moment. Stop the exchange of hurts. Ask God how you can word your truths with kindness so it can be understood.

Some people RE-act, speak with the intent to hurt so much that we subconsciously choose to be deaf to their words. Do you have someone like that in your life? Most of us do. Are you that someone in somebody's life? Let's hope not! Behavior can be changed. Just need to choose to change it. The power is within each of us to do it. Taking charge of our responses changes the journey. Our journey is built by us, with each thought/word/deed. We focus on starting with taking charge and TAKING ACTION.

We are created to ACT. Nature was created to support us in this endeavor. So, today, choose to stand your ground. Be silent when you may say something you might regret and see how much better life is!

Act in your power! Exercise self mastery! Choose not to take offense! Remember: he/she who hurts you on purpose is hurting themselves, so have compassion. Don't hurt people on purpose. When the urge comes to "let them have it!!", give it to God, He will take it if you let Him. He will help you to heal your heart. Kind words go much further than revengeful, angry and frustrated words have ever taken you. ACTION empowers the soul.

SMALL CHECK UP:

1. Am I acting or RE-acting when I speak?
2. Are my words kind? Does it feel good to think/speak them?
3. Will I regret this? Will it fuel the fire?
4. Am I communicating or defending myself?
5. Am I thinking before I speak?
6. Will this bring us closer to a solution?
7. How will my words be received? Are they fighting words or peaceful ones?

3. THERE IS ALWAYS A CHOICE

We are all born into a body which grows, ages, learns, experiences grief/joy and all the emotions in between. We are raised by some other human(s). They will feed us, change our diapers, feed or starve the nurturing which is necessary for survival and they will be our examples of how to live our lives.

Some of us are blessed and have amazing parents/families. Some are not, and some are in between. However, there is always a choice. Do we need to follow in their footsteps? If they are good, sure. If they are not, no.

This story illustrates this point well:

> *"Two boys had a father who was an alcoholic. They grew into young men. One became as his father, an*

*alcoholic. "What choice did I have?
My father was an alcoholic." The
other son was successful, had a
family and found happiness. He
never touched a drop of alcohol.
"How could I? Look what it did to
my father."*

There are always choices. No one can make you do anything. "You can lead the horse to water, but you can't make it drink."

Children who are abused need people to choose for them, to get help, to get them out of that situation. People must choose to get involved and make a change. There is always a good choice or a better choice. We need to look for it, because it is not always visible… it is always there. We cannot find them if we are not looking for them.

It serves us well to make good choices before they are placed before us. What do I mean? Be pro-active. In relationships with people that are negative, fault finding, judgmental and powerfully vocal, be prepared to think before speaking. Do not internalize whatever garbage they throw at you and focus on being kind. There are less regrets that way.

If you are changing your eating and/or exercising life style for the umpteenth time (I wouldn't know it myself - HA!) and you know what your weaknesses are, take them away. Don't have temptations in your house. Create new habits and trash the old ones, EVER DAY, one day at a time.

If you know you are a procrastinator (the struggle is real), make goals and work on them daily. I don't care if it is 5 minutes or 5 hours. Choose to achieve it! One day at a time. This book has been in the making for years in my head. Last year, I finally started writing it, and now, the typing of it. Once I started it, I set the goal to finish it by the end of the month. I was done procrastinating, it was time to get it done!

Choose good words to come from your mind out of your mouth. Choose words that build, empower and create great things. Choose to stand in light. If it is dark all around, be the light, be the higher vibration. Your choice in being that will attract the same to you. Choose to be pro-active, to make the hard choices before they show up on your path. Choose to be kind to rude people. They won't know what to do with you :) Choose to make a difference for the good. God gave us two ears and one mouth; use them in that proportion. Listen more than you speak and speak from the heart.

Choose to love yourself so you can love others. Choose to change when what you are doing is not bringing joy into your soul.

SMALL CHECK UP

1. Am I doing my best here? Is this the best choice for me?

2. Am I doing what I've been raised to do? Is that the best option for myself? Do I need to break a pattern here?

3. Is this addiction or does it brings me joy to do it?

4. Could I be happier if I choose differently? Should I learn more about it?

5. Am I acting out of fear/doubt? Am I doing this because I care what people think?

6. Is this going to bring good things into my life? Or I am just doing what everyone is doing because I want to fit in?

7. What are the consequences of this choice? Will it be beneficial?

4. LAWS

The universe was created, is run and works through laws. These are not man's laws, but God's laws. These laws you and I cannot break, cheat or ignore. What do I mean by that? The laws of God, the laws of nature are unchangeable and unbreakable.

Let's look at the law of time. Time is measured in hours. However, the most important thing to realize is that time passes. The night dawns into morning, the day comes to twilight and back into night. As time passes, we grow older, memories are made. We create the life we live, unable to go back in time. We can use it however we choose, but we cannot repeat it, change the past, or predict with certainty what will happen tomorrow. We are at the mercy of time.

We can't break the natural laws, but we can break ourselves trying… constantly. It would be nice to know what they are, so we could work with them, instead of against them. I am going to touch on just a few to give you an idea. These gems were found in the scriptures, after I learned about them through books, audio books, pod casts and life in general. There is a law for everything! Look around and see for yourself!

LAW OF GRATITUDE

It takes us to a higher frequency and vibration, in the scriptures we are told to give thanks in all things: ALL THINGS!!! When we can give thanks for everything, we are using the law of polarity. When something horrific happens we are focused enough to find the amazing in it. It takes work! But what an awesome result we get. Gratitude in all things makes life simpler and better. There is always good in everything. We need to look for and find it, so we can truly be grateful for it.

LAW OF GESTATION

We get to wait on the time that it takes to create things. i.e., surgery recovery takes time. To build a house takes time, traveling takes time, releasing weight and getting fit takes time. Building dreams takes time. Remember the law of time: it passes. What we do with our emotions about time is key to the enjoyment of the journey. Gestation is part of the process of creation.

LAW OF ACCOUNTABILITY

You may choose what you want to do, however the consequences are not yours to choose, i.e.:, you may choose to have no initiative on realizing your dream . That's fine. Just know it won't be realized. One may choose to spend all the money he makes and more. That's a sure way to be broke, all the time. We may choose to eat healthy, be active and get enough sleep. Feeling well is a great reward. Choice is ours, but we receive consequences from the laws we obeyed or tried to break, cheat, and/or ignore.

LAW OF VIBRATION

Everything that has a cell in itself vibrates. The atom vibrates. To attract the things/people/events we desire, we must vibrate at a high vibration. We must vibrate to create! Low vibration keeps you from moving higher and into light.

High vibration keeps you creating and attracting ridiculously wonderful things out of seeming thin air. Discover the law that you need to obey to obtain what you want.

LAW OF THOUGHT

One of the laws we usually break ourselves against is the law of thought. If our quiet thoughts, which can be the loudest at times, are against what we are doing, we get nowhere fast. So, do an inventory of your quietest/loudest thoughts. Are any of these occupying good space in your mind?

- What will people think/say?
- I can't do it.
- I don't deserve it.
- It is too hard.
- I am too busy.
- I am scared of…
- I am a failure, why even try?
- I am going to fail.
- I will do it tomorrow.
- I am stupid .

- What's the use?
- Nobody ever done this, it is impossible!
- Nobody love me.
- I hate myself.
- I am not enough.
- I give up, life is not worth living.
- Why me?
- I deserve being mistreated, I am nothing.
- I don't deserve love.
- I am who I am because I was born this way.
- I am a part of my family, no one has ever done this, I can't do it.
- I deserve to be abused.

Replace them with good emotions/high vibration, empowering thoughts.

- People's opinion of me is their business.
- I believe in myself, I can do hard things.
- I deserve all the blessings God grants me daily.
- Hard things help me grow. I am excited for the challenge.

- I have time and I use it wisely.
- I am fearless with God by my side.
- I am a work in progress, learning with every experience.
- I am doing my best and if it doesn't work out, I find a way to make it happen
- Today is the day I have, one step at a time, doing my best.
- That was not a wise choice, I've learned my lesson.
- I am leaning on the Lord, He uses me to do His work.
- All things are possible with God. He gave me this mountain to show the world it can be moved.
- God loves me and I love myself, that's a great start.
- I am God's creation, a miracle. I am finding one thing today that I can love about myself. (repeat that)
- I am enough. I have enough. I create, grow and empower myself with God's love for me.
- Life is beautiful! I am looking for the beauty hidden in everything. Challenge accepted!

- Why not me? I am excited to see how this turns out!
- I deserve love, I deserve respect and I deserve joy. I am a soul, an eternal being, a limitless individual.
- I am love, I love myself and I am loved by God. I deserve to be loved.
- I can/and I change myself for the better.
- My family did the best they could with what they had. I know more, I understand more, I break the cycle here, right now.
- Nobody deserves abuse, specially me, I walk away from abuse and never look back.

Thoughts are powerful!
Empower yourself with good ones! :)

LAW OF EMOTIONS

Emotions rule our perception of things. Two people can have the same exact experience and take away two completely different, if not opposite, perceptions. As in the quote about the twin boys who had an alcoholic father... one of the boys grew up to be just like his father because he felt he had no choice on the matter. The other chose the complete opposite because of the example of their father. One felt he had no choice on the matter, the misery was too great for the other to continue in it. The emotions we attach to events will create the path we walk. When fearful, we face incredible challenges to make us even more scared. When positive and hopeful, alike people will show up along the way and events that are happy and positive are created collectively. When angry, be prepared to encounter the same emotion in your world. All consuming and hurtful.

Choose the emotions you keep. Watch for them! They define your thoughts. Only feed the thoughts with emotions that do the heart good.

LAW OF LIGHT
We all have light, we should shine it as bright as we know how! Light is life, God is light and light is the law that runs the universe.

Here are some of the emotions that are light bringers: love, caring, peace, joy, empowerment, delight, positive attitude, integrity, character. All these feel good to the heart; that which brings peace is of light. The brighter we shine, the better the world becomes around us. People need light for their spirit; the world is dark. We are to shine as bright as we can to help ourselves and those around us. Light is the law that rules the universe. Light brings hope to everyone.

LAW OF DARKNESS

Darkness is the absence of light. It can drag down a soul really low and take the desire for living away. Darkness is the opposite of light. It doesn't run the universe, it vibrates low and stops people from doing and being their best.

Darkness helps us to appreciate the light and long for it. Darkness is powerful when it infiltrates the mind and heart. Don't go there, it is often times very hard to get out of it.

LAW OF POLARITY

The bigger the tragedy, the bigger the greatness. Look for the good in every bad thing. It is there! You just have to look for it and find it. The more powerless you feel, the more power is within you to drawn upon and to act from. The more fearful you are about something awful, the deeper courage of a warrior is awaiting to be awakened and marched with.

The tragedies we have seen in history are unimaginable, however, have you heard the story of the survivors? Have you seen the faith, courage, knowledge, wisdom, love with which they walked away? If you are at a tough spot where it is overwhelming to get out of bed, start looking for the good, the lesson, the strength hidden in your heart. Go find it! Use it and enjoy it!

LAW OF FORGIVENESS

When we truly forgive, we set ourselves free. We let go of the weight of all the negativity we've been carrying around. It is like whatever you wish happens to that individual stays in you. Yuck!

"Resentment is like drinking poison and then hoping it will kill your enemies."

—Nelson Mandela

Forgiveness allows us to grow, to truly let go and to change behavior. Sometimes we are the hardest on ourselves for wrong doings. The law of time doesn't allow us to go change the past, I wish we could, but we can't. We can however, learn from it and not do it again.

Holding people hostage in not forgiving them, hurts us more than it hurts them. Sure, we may take away things, people they hold dear, but they will somehow go on with life and if you are not forgiving, you may create health issues for yourself because of the bitterness you choose to house in your body. Be mindful. Be prayerful. Bring out the divine in you, forgive.

LAW OF ABUNDANCE

To be abundant we cannot think with a scarcity mind. To connect to God's abundance, we need to work on believing we are worthy of it and choose the company we keep. Like minded people do like minded things. Give thanks for all that you already have and for what you are about to receive, use it wisely and share.

God's abundance is infinite. We are His children, heirs of it all. However, if we don't think we are worthy of it, that we are born poor and poor we shall die, He doesn't interfere with choice. Agency is the only thing we have that is ours to claim.

Abundance has to be chosen, looked for and received, with gratitude to the Giver of it. Give thanks for the abundance that you already have. Abundance of health, faith, energy, love, food, clothing, you know… everything.

LAW OF RELEASE

Nothing is ours to keep. In Brazil ,we have a saying "caskets don't carry drawers," meaning, we don't take anything with us when we die. Nothing and no one is our possession. People specially, we tend to say my spouse, my father/ my mother, my children/grandchildren. Yes, we are related to them one way or another, however, they are not ours.

We have the privilege to raise children, but they are their own persons and they will build their own lives. Spouses are our partners through life, but they are their own individual soul, created by

God. Don't take possession of what is not yours. Release! No jealousy, no strings attached, no conditions, no anything. People are born free and free they should exist.

Relationships that are filled with conditions, threats, insecurities and jealousies are unhealthy and unsuccessful. The law of release is to completely live free and give freedom to loved ones. Not on you what they do with it. But on you to give it to them.

LAW OF "I AM"

"I AM" are the two most powerful words on the planet. Whatever we put behind it and repeat often (even casually) sticks. Make sure what goes after I AM is good! Make sure it is positive and empowering: it has the power to override the limiting beliefs we have created, inherited or picked up. Be so very mindful of how you use this law. It literally creates who you are.

Remember to not say you are what you did. What do I mean? You may have done something incredibly dumb, that action doesn't make you dumb, it was dumb to do it. You are not fat permanently, you can change that, so, instead of "I AM fat", how about "I AM making different choices for my body, I am working at releasing weight and getting fit." You get the point.

LAW OF FAITH

We all have heard "faith precedes the miracle." But we don't observe that law as much as we should. Faith stretches us to trust God with our living, it teaches us to follow promptings, empowers us to take one more step in the climb of our lives, it unites us, helps us through everything and anything.

Faith teaches us about forgiveness for the most awful things, understanding of the most painful behavior and compassion for the children of God. With faith comes miracles. Exercise faith, doubting not and waiting on God's timing.

Faith helps us to not be so attached to the outcome. Exercise faith and watch what God does with our small effort. Blessings we didn't know we needed will show up out of nowhere at the perfect time and place.

If you are working on a dream or goal (dream with a deadline), find the law you need to obey to bring it to pass. There are laws for everything! They can't be broken, let us not break ourselves against them.

Laws of God, laws of nature are eternal and they exist to help us to fulfill our potential. God is bound by them as we are. Our part on obeying them is so small compared to what they bring upon us as we are blessed with the promise in them.

We are children of God. He is the Father of us all. He knows from beginning to end. He knows what we will choose, and we are responsible for our choices. His plan is big enough to fit all of our journeys and all the detours we take along the way.

SMALL CHECK UP:

1. Do I know the law that I need to observe right now?

2. Am I obeying the law for this desired blessing?

3. What law am I not observing? There is so much going wrong!

4. Are my thoughts good?

5. Are my words kind?

6. What law can I learn today?

7. How can I share what I've learned and benefit others on their journey?

5. FEAR

Fear is as powerful as we let it be. The tricky part is that fear almost always is logical or seems to makes sense. Satan uses fear to keep us from moving forward, doing things that will make the world a better place and loving unconditionally.

Also, fear of success is a real thing. We say and think consciously we want to succeed, but inside we fear how to keep up success and how to obtain it. What is going to cost us. Fear shows up in many ways and we don't realize how powerful we allow it to be. Someone may say, "you can't do this, it has never been done." And boom! It makes sense! It has never been done, so, I probably can't do it! Then the fear and doubt sets in. I am thankful that great inventors didn't believe a silly statement like that.

If it makes your soul burn with excitement, keeps your mind working in a way you can accomplish it and it is all you can do to not jump for joy as you build it in your mind, THEN IT CAN BE DONE AND YOU ARE THE ONE TO DO IT!!!!

How about when you try to do something and it doesn't work, you embarrass yourself in the attempt and you get to do it again? Or your family and friends think you are nuts for trying?

Maybe you go to a party you only know the host? Or, the doctor just told you that you have a bad disease… and you believe him 100%? Or the loss of a job? Or you graduated college and "now what?" Maybe you've lost a loved one? Moved away and don't know a soul because you ended a relationship and here you are, at a brand new start, alone? Becoming a parent? Getting married? Your children are all grown up and you hope the correct principles you've taught them are enough for them to find happiness in their lives? Need to communicate something to the person that always twists what you say?

Fear is born in the first doubt that comes up; it is up to us to feed it and let it grow or starve it and make it die. We usually create more doubts to feed it. I found that to get rid of fear, I have to give it to the Lord EVERY SINGLE TIME! It makes fear less powerful and faith stronger. Only God can give and bring peace to the mind and heart. Fear does the opposite: it takes sleep away, it makes us agitated and insecure.

FEAR: unworthy of a Child of God. Uneasiness of mind, the passion of our nature which excites us to provide for our security, on the approach of evil. We fear the approach of an enemy or of a storm.

FAITH: a principal of action and power, and by it one can command the elements, heal the sick, and influence any number of circumstances when occasion warrants. All true faith must be based upon correct knowledge or it cannot produce the desired results. The assent of the mind or understanding to the truth of what God has revealed.

God inspires people on the daily basis, the more we follow the promptings, the more He can trust us with more impressions. We shall overcome fear with faith and love.

- Fear can be paralyzing.
- Faith can give us wings.
- Fear keeps us from speaking truths.
- Faith turns up our voices to empower humanity with truths.
- Fear is a dark/low vibration negative emotion.
- Faith is a bright/high vibration and positive empowerment from the Creator of mankind.
- Fear keeps us from doing what we must do to grow, love and become our potential and fulfill our life mission.
- Faith carries us through the storm, help us to keep on moving forward, open our hearts to love and be loved, quiets the doubts that feed fear and help us to fulfill our life mission and return to God.
- Fear is not worthy of me or anyone else.
- Faith empowers everyone.

Let us work on letting go of fear, rebuking it from our minds and let us embrace the courage faith brings, unleash the soul to soar in the love and light of God.

SMALL CHECK UP

1. Why am I reluctant to do this? Is it fear?
2. How much am I listening to people's opinions of my actions? Do I feel encouraged?
3. Can I be excited about this? Am all in?
4. Do I feel peace? Would including God in this help?
5. Am I playing small because I am fearful I will fail?
6. If I knew it would work out in the end, would I start?
7. What is the good that can come out of this?

6. EMOTIONS ARE POWERFUL

*"We do not attract what we want,
but what we are."*

—James Lane Allen

What we focus on, what we fear, what we keep on doubting, what we say to ourselves in the quiet of our thoughts and what we truly are is what we create in our day to day lives. IT IS TIME TO POLICE THE MIND AND HEART! Pay attention!

Almost nine years ago, I was able to set up a five generation picture. That took my mom coming from Brazil, my grandma coming from Vashon, WA to be with myself, my daughter and her brand new baby boy here in Utah. The emotions in that room were powerful! A brand new mom with her babe, a first time nana, a great grandma and a great, great grandma were together for the first time. The cycles of life in that moment were wrapped in the love for the children.

The love of each mother for their own child and their child's child...repeat. This is a great memory full of positive emotion and a picture that cannot be repeated. Do you have anger, frustration, doubt, loneliness, hurt, offenses, judgments of self and others? The low vibration, negative, dark emotions? If you expect, focus on being broke, even when extra money shows up because you put some effort into changing, something will break and you will spend it on fixing it.

Or when you are angry at someone because they offended you, you will find more and more reason to be angry, to not forgive. Then it consumes your peace, calmness and health. In my opinion, that is a waste of energy and time.

How about when you hope a relationship will work, but you keep focusing on the reasons why it shouldn't? Indeed, it won't. Emotions are powerful!

Here are some emotions that are shifters for the good to happen in your life. Give thanks for what you desire before you have it. Be descriptive!

Example:
"I am grateful for all the copies this book is selling as it is done, published and on line. I give thanks that through my schooling of hard knocks, I am able to learn how to heal myself with God.

I am grateful I am better for my schooling. I am thankful I get to speak about this book and the other books I've written to help people be whole again, have hope and move forward one step at a time. And I see it!

I am grateful we can collectively raise vibration all over the globe because fear is everywhere, and that is enough of it! I am excited to help individuals and families to overcome fear and doubts.

I am very grateful and excited for the healing I have experienced myself, how empowering it has been in my life and how God can empower others through me. I don't know all the people reading this book, yet, we connect through these words!

I am grateful for my faith and my relationship with God. I have escaped paralysis caused by fear and despair. I am so grateful I've turned my light as bright as it goes and now as it burns, I am a light bringer into the darkness of the world. That makes my heart so happy!

I am giving thanks for all the trials/tough crap I had to go through to figure things out and come out much better on the other side. Looking and finding joy along the way. I am truly grateful for all the tears I've cried; in the last 5 years I've cried more than I have in my 53 years combined and I lived to tell the tale. I kept on waking up every morning and somehow gotten through every impossible day.

I am so excited and very grateful for the beautiful place I call home, where I feel safe, happy, peaceful, I feel the Spirit of God, joy and it is a place of gathering. I give thanks for my businesses that I was fearful of creating, now I am relentless in building. It is important; God told me so. I am far from my comfort zone and all in! It feels amazing!

People whom I needed to get it going showed up, ways were created and I am enjoying the journey. I am grateful for all the traveling I do! I travel for work and pleasure, to speak healing to the world that so sorely needs it! "

Just so you know, as I am writing the book, the businesses are starting and I am not living at the place I described it. However, I visualize it several times a day, all of it, as if I already have it and am enjoying it: every single day, several times a day. The people are showing up, as God said they would if I started putting one foot in front of the other to get it done. So I dragged my feet…for years :(and now, here we are, going God speed, which, due to my procrastination, is going fast right now :)

Have gratitude for the good things that are coming your way! Be emotional about it! Several times a day, every day! Emotions tell on you and me. What we feel, regardless if we speak it out loud or not is going to show up/be created right before our eyes because we feed it in our thoughts, which create the life we live.

GRATITUDE + GOOD EMOTIONS
+ INSPIRED WORK + TRUST IT IS
HAPPENING = COMPLETE CHANGE.

PLEASE DON'T LET PEOPLE CONTROL
HOW YOU FEEL! ABOUT SELF, LIFE,
CREATIVITY, LOVE...ALL THE THINGS
THAT ARE UP TO YOU TO CREATE AND
ENJOY!

Other people's opinions of your life are for them to keep and for you to ignore. Always go back to the why you desire and the intensity of the good emotions attached to it. Make room for it! Hop on the opportunities that show up from thin air. Delete fear from your vocabulary of thought and speech.

- Be brave because you fed courage.
- Be in the moment!
- Be limitless in imagining/ creating/ enjoying the dream as it builds itself!
- Love with your whole heart! There are less regrets that way.
- Give your all to whatever cause matters to you.

- Learn the lesson, forgive the pain, let go of it.
- Communicate with kindness, we are all working hard at living the best we can.
- Turn to God every time. He will show you the way, give you strength, love you unconditionally, bless you, perform miracles after your exercise the faith.

EMOTION Definition: Literally, a moving of the mind or soul, hence, any agitation of mind or excitement of sensibility. Be positively, powerfully emotional and grateful about your desires! Be consistent and persistent! Watch your world change! The impossible makes you smile. You know better, you are doing it, you are creating it from/with/through your heart! Emotions make things happen. Try it out! Positive as if you have it, with plenty contentment, always grateful and always welcome!

SMALL CHECK UP

1. Am I feeling it from the heart? Am I focusing on it?
2. Does it make me so excited, it is hard not to work on it all the time?

3. What emotion could I add to this? To make it more exciting.

4. Am I just going through the motions? What do I need to change?

5. Are my emotions positive or negative? How can I better them?

6. How will I feel when I finally accomplish this? I am pumped!

7. Is my goal big enough that it will change me for the better in the process?

7. WE ALL MAKE MISTAKES, GET OVER IT

L ife is made of choices. We choose the best option with the knowledge we have at the time. Period. Hind sight is 20/20. Don't resent or regret anything on that account. What we would've done if we knew then what we know now - we cannot change what we did then. We can't live in the past or from the past. It doesn't work.

Life is simple, made up of choices that are made from beliefs and emotions on which we focus. We make choices daily, some are excellent, some are ok and some are simply not the best choice. We react a lot instead of taking action. We allow people's words and actions affect how we feel about life, or worse, ourselves. We choose popularity instead of values. We treat people according to economic classes. We are easily hurt for nothing or we take offense too easily. We exercise less faith and lots of doubt. We make choices that are easy instead the hard ones. Yes, the list is way longer…

We ALL make mistakes! Guaranteed! We hurt people unintentionally and are a lot of times unaware of what we are doing. Society has standards of right and wrong, we have values. Going against our values/character to please society is a very dangerous way of living.

MISTAKE: to take wrong; to conceive or understand erroneously; to misunderstand or misapprehend. To err in option or judgment. God has commanded us to be perfect.

PERFECT: fully developed, complete, finished. NOT flawless, without mistakes and errors.

I am so very grateful I can forgive as quickly as the thought enters my mind and offense/ hurt doesn't have power over me. If it grabs me for a moment, I recognize it, cry over it, give thanks for it and give it to God.

It is getting easier and I do it faster than before. I refuse to spend precious energy on things that do not empower my light/energy/ vibration.

Resentment is tough to carry and powerful enough to destroy relationships. It consumes the individual from inside out. It changes behavior and it is quick to create unhappiness. BE AWARE!!!

WE REGRESS WHEN WE RESENT!

Own your mistakes and try to fix them. Ask for forgiveness of the person, of self and ultimately of God when you make mistakes. When you've done all that you can, LET IT GO! Some people will hold it over your head for life. It is Ok, if you've done all you can, you should have peace about it; God gives you that. After that, there is nothing else that you can do. Their choice to hold it over your head is not in your power to change. You choose to keep walking and applying the lessons learned - PROGRESS.

On the same token, don't be the one holding people's mistakes over their heads. The lesson was theirs to learn. You've got enough of your own to work on; don't waste precious time "holding people accountable." Take care of your own accountability. Every parent of multiple children will tell you they became better parents as each child came along. Unfortunately, their first child will be the teacher of parenting. Most of the mistakes will happen to them. Sad, but true. I wish I knew what I know now when I was raising my kids. I am grateful I raised them with better insight than my parents raised me and my hope is that they will raise their children better than they were raised.

We all are going to error one way or another. Stressing over is silly, just understand we are not perfect and we will make mistakes. GET OVER IT!

Mistakes come packed with good lessons. Look for those, so when the opportunity comes up, you can do better and produce happier results.

SMALL CHECK UP

1. Am I being too hard on people and self for mistakes we made?

2. Am I being a perfectionist? Are my expectations too high?

3. Have I been merciful to self and others?

4. Does this needs improvement? How can I do it?

5. Do I need to use different words to express myself? More positive?

6. Do I need to ask for forgiveness?

7. Do I need to forgive and let go?

8. THE SCHOOL OF HARD KNOCKS

Have you learned many things the hard way, by choice? I have. This small book is a small part of what I have learned. Being a parent, your first child gets to be the Guinea pig for your parenting. No manual included, no re-do, no amount of preparation can get you ready to be a parent. You learn as you go.

I used to say I like learning things the hard way, I guess that's what I did. I remember when I started doing energy work and I didn't know how much to charge, I went up and down with the price and did it for free for a while. Funny thing, when people are not invested, they don't value the work. After much trial and error, I charged for my time, and people started valuing the work and doing their homework. I also have learned that a lot of people are looking for a

Band Aid and support in being miserable. I have fired myself from working on them. I learned it the hard way at the time, but it sure stuck.

Getting into a romantic relationship has challenges. When things get serious...sometimes we cruise through it and sometimes we crash and burn. Either way, we live through it and come out better on the other side. How about people. Have you been cheated by someone you trusted 100%? Have you been used? Have you been the point of gossip because you've trusted someone with something really private? Have you believed liars? Have you helped people because you cared and then turn around and have them take the credit? Have you ever been "abandoned"?

We all have had some hard knocks along the way. The good thing about the school of hard knocks is that the lesson usually sticks! And if we apply the lesson to life with gladness, we are not doomed to repeating what got taught us in the first place. What we've learned from experience carries emotion - charged emotion! It moves us! It helps us grow and become stronger, more savvy, trust worthy, faithful, courageous, daring, loving, kinder… all of the good that can come from disaster or storms with no end in sight.

However sometimes people become bitter, angry, frustrated, vengeance seekers, judgmental… the ugly and yucky stuff. Usually the older you get, the more of what/who you really are shows through.

What do I mean? If you have a kind heart, have found joy for most of your life and done good with the things you came across, then you live in peace and are peaceful. You have light in your soul, which you share and you are happy wherever life has taken you and however you are living it.

When someone chooses bitter over happy, judgment over peace, resentment over forgiveness, jealousy over joy… they will have misery to share in abundance, negativity to be spoken day and night and will be very unhappy with the life they live, anywhere they are. There is a saying :

**"If you can't be a good example,
don't be a terrible warning."**

It is a true statement, and it gives us insight.

Take a look back at life. Look for the hard times and in that, look for the sweetness of the lesson. It's bitter sweet, but we get to go on and add wisdom to the journey.

- Not everyone believes in honor, honesty and trust.
- Not everyone has morals.
- Not everyone cares.
- Not everyone follows through .
- Not everyone will deliver what they promise.
- Not everyone deserves your time.
- Not everyone is capable of loving deeply.

We are to live with honor, being honest and worthy of trust. It makes life brighter and better. Being moral helps us to have a good compass and to make life with less drastic ups and downs. When we care, we become an instrument in God's hands and we see/are a part of blessings and miracles . Being a finisher is rare and absolutely wonderful! We accomplish things and the world becomes a better place. Delivering whatever we promised is powerful.

There is so much empowerment in honoring our word. Time is precious, spend it wisely. We cannot change the past, throw money at it to stop it from passing or repeat the moment. Be wise on how and with whom you spend your time.

Oh my heart! Not everyone can love you as much as you can love them. Most people guard their heart behind thick, tall and deep walls. They are afraid of getting hurt. Remember, love is a beautiful and powerful emotion/verb that not everyone is capable of doing. Understanding that we all have had some school of hard knocks and learning from it is the first stepping stone to get a better view of the path we are on and make decisions accordingly.

Look for the joy in your journey. It makes it all worth it. Welcome to the school of hard knocks! It enables us to create an amazing life or a very deep valley in which to live. Let it teach you the lesson and let it help you create a journey worthy of joy!

SMALL CHECK UP

1. Am I bitter or better for the experience?
2. Is life a blessing or do I feel cursed?
3. Do I trust the outcome is just what I need?
4. Am I looking for the lesson, so I can learn it?
5. Am I a good example or a terrible warning?
6. Do I look at things from different perspectives or just mine?
7. Have I enjoyed the experience I have gained?

9. FOCUS, IT IS IMPORTANT

I meditate morning and night. It has been so helpful! I am visualizing things happening and I add emotion to it. There are small things coming to pass and I can feel the big ones getting closer. I focus on the events and places that matter to me with my full attention. During the day, I visualize it in my mind's eye and when any doubt, discouragement, fear that tries to sneak in, I quickly get rid of it and focus even more on the visualization. I focus on a healthy body, abundance, peace, love, freedom, joy, my businesses I am creating, this book I am soon publishing... And I am becoming aware of the obstacles and getting rid of them. I am also aware of my thinking and changing it when necessary. Last but not least, I am aware of the small and great opportunities that show up...I've taken every one of them.

On what do you focus? Do you focus on the goals or the fears of failing to achieve them? Where does your mind wander to when you don't have to think of anything? What does your life look like? You either created with your thoughts/ deeds/words or you attracted with your thoughts/deeds/words. Believe me, I don't like some of the things I've created. I'm not ashamed to admit it. I did, however, learn that I can change it.

We usually focus on the things we fear or don't want. And we get to deal with it as it becomes our reality:

- Do you look for and focus on the good in people, things and events?
- Do you look for solutions or do you give the problem more depth and power?
- Do you try to enjoy the day or do you have an "Eeyore" attitude?
- Do you bring faith in your heart or fear in your mind?
- Do you focus on the goal or all of the obstacles why you shouldn't even try?

- Are you obsessed in a good way with what you desire to create?

Do you let a pebble on your path stop you from finishing the journey? Pebbles can be stepped over, rocks give you a better view if you use it as a stepping stone to see what is ahead and bolders develop muscles or the ability to go over, around it or explode it out of the way. To some, a pebble is all it takes to destroy focus. Don't let it be you! A pebble sinks into the ground if you step on it. No other thought should be given to it!

WHAT I FOCUS ON, I CREATE!

Read it again! What is your focus right now? What are you focusing on as physical health goes?

Are you saying:

- I am sick.
- I don't feel good.
- I am scared of diseases.
- I am fat and unhealthy.

- I am dying of _____.
- My doctor said I am sick; I am scared.
- It is genetics, I can't change it.

OR, are you focusing on:

- I am getting better.
- I am feeling better
- I have a strong immune system.
- I am getting fit.
- I am living today, making the day count, I am safe, my immune system works well!
- I am trusting God and listening to inspiration.
- I can change my DNA if I chose to do so.

When we focus on good things, the mind will help us to do things that are good for us. When we focus on bad things, our minds will take us to the results of our thinking.

BE AWARE OF YOUR FOCUS!
YOUR LIFE COMES FROM WHERE YOU MIND GOES!

How about your financial health?

- I am always broke,
- There is not enough $ to pay the bills.
- I can't have fun, there is not money.
- I make little money, never enough.
- I can't own a business; no one in my family has.
- I hate my job.
- I am a failure.

OR

- My income is increasing.
- I am open to financial opportunities .
- I am open to and welcome a different job.
- I am creating a passive income.
- I am the boss of me, I am a business owner.
- I am successful in my endeavors.

How is your relationship health?

- Are you the person with whom you want to be in a relationship?
- Are you worthy of trust?
- Are you kind, caring, loving?
- Are you selfless?

- Are you spiritual? (if you desire it in someone else)
- Are you happy by yourself?
- Are you positive, empowering and light?

We definitely are with the person who is comfortable to be with because of who we are. Some of us may say, "YAY!" And some of us may say, "OUCH!" If you want to change the relationship you are in, GREAT! Change yourself.

- Stop reacting - take action.
- Stop waiting - start doing.
- Stop waiting to be asked - offer help.
- Stop getting offended - forgive and communicate better.
- Stop expecting - start speaking for yourself.
- Stop criticizing - start listening to understand, not to reply.
- Find out their love language, use it.
- Take mental notes of wishes, dreams, wants and bucket lists - deliver as you can.
- Make them a priority - make time, talk.

- Make them feel special.
- Focus on making things better, great, best!
- Honor yourself so you can honor them .
- Teach by example how you want to be treated.
- Communicate clearly - make sure you are understood in the things that really matter to you.
- Communication starts in the thoughts of your mind and heart.
- Communicate well within yourself.
- Get focused and get it done.

SMALL CHECK UP

1. What do I focus on when I wake up?
2. Where does my mind wander to when I don't have to think?
3. Are my thoughts uplifting or dragging me down?
4. Do I focus on the obstacles or the possibilities?
5. Do I consider myself an open minded person?
6. Do I focus on the goal or the negativity from people around me?
7. Am I all in on the pursuit of joy in my life? If not, what is stopping me?

10. BOUNDARIES ARE HEALTHY

Do you feel like people have more power over you than you would like them to have? Or, they have too much say in your life? Even if you don't utilize what they say, they speak too much into your doings?

BOUNDARIES ARE HEALTHY!

BOUNDARY: a limit. A visible mark designating a limit.

This "line" is where you stop! Draw it in your mind, heart, ground…but draw the line and that is where the buck stops!

Family and close friends are the hardest with whom to have boundaries. I was a sucker for no boundaries. People had the ability to walk all over me. And I, in return, would lay flat so they could. I was a doormat, if you will.

Boundaries are necessary if we are to live a healthy life. Respecting the boundaries does us all a lot of good. How do you know what boundaries to set? Here are some of the healthy reasons to set boundaries:

- When you don't feel safe.
- When you are afraid of the reactions of people towards you.
- When people constantly take advantage of you.
- When you feel disrespected.
- When people use you to get things for themselves.
- When you give and give, but it is not a two way street.
- When you do your job and theirs for no extra money.
- When they only spend time with you when they have no other options . Now you may ask, "How do I build boundaries?" You don't allow people to overstep clearly

drawn lines. You stop them. What does it take? How does it work? Listen to what they say and when it is headed the way it shouldn't, stop them before it gets there. In your mind, in your energy set the intention , "I AM SAFE", "I am beyond their reach, I am owning my energy field, I am protected."

Some people are masters at ignoring boundaries: become a master at implementing them.

"Boundaries are, in simple terms, the recognition of personal space."

—Asa Don Brown

I was in a very toxic relationship, I was willing to change, but the other person wasn't. And in their eyes/mind, I was never good enough. They were negative and very critical my whole life. It caused years of despair, frustration, and at one point, deep suicidal depression. You ask, "Why didn't you end the relationship?" I couldn't:

I didn't know how. I didn't know I could. So, thanks to a friend's help, I went to counseling. There, I learned so many things!

- I am in charge of how far or how close people get to me.

- My beliefs: spiritual, emotional, physical and mental are mine to keep and preserve. If anyone disrespects them, it is up to me alone to say NO, STOP, THIS IS NOT OK, LEAVE ME ALONE. If all fails, it is up to me to get up and walk away, hang up the phone, block the caller, delete the email or stop the frenzy in the social media post.

- Know where my limit is and stand for it - EVERY TIME!

- Speak up for myself, when people are pushing - It is OK to push back.

- Recognize that the uncomfortable part of this is a small price to pay for the peace that it brings.

- My energy field is my personal space - I connect to people with it. People are not allowed in it in an invasive way.

- I am in charge of my feelings. It is up to me to take back the power I've given people to make me feel this or that way. BOUNDARIES ARE HEALTHY!
- I respect people's boundaries as much as I want mine to be respected.
- Be aware of old habits and develop new ones. Create new behaviors.
- Be extra vigilant around those that walk all over you, or even just a little bit. Put up your "keep off sign".
- It is hard to start, but once you start, don't stop. People will learn your boundaries, relationships will become much healthier, more respectful and kinder.
- Boundaries are a form of self love and self respect. Create them on demand and demand they are respected. You are worth it and worthy of it.

Boundaries are healthy when they protect us and help relationships to be better, more respectful and more empowering instead of draining. As I wrote earlier about the boundaries that I couldn't set in the toxic relationship, and it almost drove me to suicide decades ago, we need to respect ourselves enough to set healthy boundaries. Life becomes better and more enjoyable.

Learn the word "NO". If you can't say it, start with shaking your head "NO". If you don't stand up for yourself, no one else will. They don't know when they need to and they are too busy living their own lives.

Set boundaries and make them work. Stand up for them and enjoy the outcome!

SMALL CHECK UP

1. Are people taking advantage of me? Do I need boundaries in this relationship?
2. Am I safe with this person? Is my heart safe?
3. Am I being respected?
4. Am I able to keep my dignity in this relationship?
5. How can I keep from feeling attacked?
6. What should I change?
7. Am I giving too many people power over me?

11. PERSPECTIVE

What I see and what you see can be as opposite as the North and South Pole and just as right as rain. That's right!

PERSPECTIVE: pertaining to the science of optics; optical. To see.

We see things how we feel, we feel according to our experiences and way of thinking. We are unique that way. Here is an example: There are two people, one is a history buff, the other a romantic. If they were to watch a movie that involved romance and war, to what do you think they would be paying attention? The one would be fact checking the history and the other would be paying attention to the love story. Is one right and one wrong? NO! Just very different perspectives. Same movie, just different optics.

How about relationships? Love language plays a big part. We tend to do things how we would like, not how the other person would - Pay Attention! Communication is key. So many arguments happen because of miscommunication. Sometimes we say something innocent that we think is kind, but the other person hears criticism and judgment. Make sure you are saying what you want to say in a way that it is understood.

Things are not always what they seem to be. Be observant and ask smart questions.People will put up a good front to be left alone. If you care, look for their perspective on things; you might be able to help express yourself better.

Perspective is truth wrapped in emotions. There are many roads to the same destination. There are many different ways to see a situation. There are many ways to express yourself. There are many ways to arrive at the ideal solution for the same problem.

PERSPECTIVE!

Respect other's perspectives as you would like yours to be respected. Yes, what you send out comes back to you. Right now there is a divide in the world of politics, to say the least. At the time of this writing, it is November 2021. There is a mandate on people to get a vaccine for Covid 19.

The perspectives are:

- Get vaccinated so if you get sick it won't be as bad.
- Get vaccinated so you protect high risk people.
- Get vaccinated to have herd immunity.
- Get vaccinated to be able to go places and work.

Now the flip side:

- People who have had Covid have natural immunity.
- Mandates on health are not ok.
- The vaccine is not proven safe, people taking it are the experiment.
- There are far more complications from the vaccine than what is being reported.

I know people in both sides, and I, myself, took a side. However, each person is in charge of their perspective and what they do with it. It saddens me to see the divide that the politicians created in the world. In Germany, we are seeing history repeat itself, not with a star to show, but vaccine passports.

Perspective.

It is up to us to educate ourselves on whatever it is of interest so we can have a solid, feel good, best for self perspective. Remember - the way we see/think things, is how things happen.

People will do things that are out of our control, and yet, they affect us deeply. Perspective can unite or divide, look at the world from 2020 - 2022 (it is now January 2022 as I type this chapter), the things that people did/are doing to each other because of masks, vaccine or natural immunity. Wow! Division worldwide.

How we see people… we don't know what they've been through and how come they are who they are because of it. The choices they saw or the roads they traveled in the circumstances placed before them. They too, don't know ours. We are individuals with individuality. Our optics are unique to each of our lives.

Keep in mind - Your perspective was created from your mind and heart. Keep learning, you may change it. Stand for it, it is important to the soul.

SMALL CHECK UP

1. Am open to different perspectives?
2. Is my perspective valid? Is there a better one out there?
3. Am I understanding of other perspectives?
4. Can I give thanks for different perspectives?
5. Is my perspective emotionally healthy?
6. Did I get this perspective in light or fear?
7. Do I honor my perspective?

12. BE A MAGNET OF GOOD THINGS

I used to be a very negative person. Yup, you've read that right. I also attracted negativity, low vibration and low self esteem. Now a days, I am as positive as I can muster to be. When I am out and about, I smile at people, wish them a good day, wave at little ones who keep staring at me, speak positive words to those with whom I am in touch and I am always glad to see my day become fabulous because of my attitude.

High vibration emotions attract high vibrating events, people and places. To be a magnet of good things we must have good things inside of us. We truly attract/create what/who we are.

Read it again. To attract health, we must have thoughts that support/create health. What do I mean? What do you think we will create if we constantly think, speak and act like this:

- I don't feel good.
- I am sick.
- I am tired.
- The doctor said I have_____.
- I am dying.
- I hate my body.
- I hate my life.
- I am my DNA.

Those kind of thoughts, words spoken are very limiting, and, very powerful! If one tells themselves they don't feel good, they will definitely feel worse. Would you consider this instead?

"Everyday in every way I'm getting better and better."

—Emile Coul

OR

- I am feeling better today than I did yesterday.
- Life is good and getting better.
- My body is recovering.

- My health is improving.
- The symptoms are going away.
- I am healthier.

If you are not feeling well, these statements will get the mind working on starting to heal the body. It will help you to think/create a way to healing. People will show up in your life who can help you. You will learn something, read or hear exactly what you need.

I believe I will die when God sees fit, not a minute earlier or a second late. No doctor is going to tell me when that is: they don't know! And yet, when it is our time, it just happens. I absolutely disagree with terminal diagnosis with a date. However, if we accept it and live life expecting to fulfill it, we definitely will create that date of death. To me, those deadlines are changeable if we are teachable. Diseases can be healed in a DNA level. Your brain is magnificent; use it, empower it and change your life.

BE A MAGNET OF GOOD THINGS

A lot of people feel/are broke, and when extra money comes into their lives, an unexpected expense comes along with it. Have you experience that? I know I have! It is very frustrating!

Part of being a magnet of good things has to do with what we truly believe, how grateful we are and our focus, which will raise or lower our vibration. Look around. What kind of vibration is being sent out by the circle you are a part of?

When we start vibrating higher, our friends may change, it happens naturally, with ease and grace. People fall out as new people come in. Why, you ask? Because people are uncomfortable with higher vibration than theirs and higher vibration cannot help but connect to higher vibration friends. The same can happen when we are vibrating low and friends start to vibrate higher, they leave, or we do, because it is uncomfortable.

This happens when we shift to a higher more positive energy; we are pulled by others onto the same path. A magnet of good things attracts and is attracted to greater things/people/ events. We must drop the anchors that hold us back. As we do, we learn to walk faster, run, and eventually fly to our destination, our tribe and the infinite possibilities out there. Attract what your dreams are made of because you are changing yourself to live them! Here are some of the anchors that are holding you back:

- I doubt it can be done.
- I am not worthy of it.
- I fear I'll fail.
- I've tried and it didn't work.
- What will people say/think of me?
- My family won't allow me to do it.
- I don't have what it takes.
- I don't deserve success.
- I am afraid of success: it may change who I am.

Growth is never found in the comfort zone. Change never comes if there is no difference in action. Dreams are never realized if we never start. How about believing it can be done and you are the one doing it? You will have to do things you have never done before. Why? Because it changes the outcome.

Yes! You are worthy of it! You are a child of God! There are majestic things in store for you if you only believe, expect and accept it when they show up. Fear is not of God, and failure is just a way it doesn't work. Usually, it comes packed with lessons and valuable insight for the next time you try. Keep looking, keep at it, be obsessed with getting it done and you will attract a way out of thin air. Failure is a teacher, period. Don't hate it. Don't give up because of it, learn the lesson and move forward from it knowing more.

Keep on trying different ways until you find the one that works for you. Critics usually criticize because someone is doing what they are afraid to do or have tried, failed and stopped trying. So, keep in mind, "People's opinions of me are none of my business."

To be a magnet of good things, we must change by leaving the comfort zone, taking action and starting right now! We put one foot in front of the other, take one moment at a time, and do our best as we learn. We all can be magnets of good things. Life is filled with miracles for those that with faith magnetize themselves to find, attract and live them. Be one!

SMALL CHECK UP

1. Do my thoughts match my dreams?
2. What is surrounding me? Is it positive, high vibrating?
3. Do I give up too easily?
4. Am I learning the lessons in unsuccessful tries?
5. Am I out of my comfort zone?
6. Am I transforming as I work on realizing my dreams?
7. Do I need to change my circle?

13. GRIEF: IT HURTS

People process grief differently. Some take longer than others. It is nobody's business to tell someone how to grieve, how long nor how often they should grieve.

GRIEF: the pain of mind produced by loss, misfortune, injury or evils of any kind; sorrow; regret.

People feel loss differently. My experience has been to recognize the reason of my grief, feel all of it, mourn it, and give it to God. Sounds cold? I don't think so, hear me out. Grief strikes us when we least expect, and if not acknowledged, it can take us down hard!

Let me share two experiences I had in 2020. My father had a brain tumor for the past five years. It changed the man I knew, and I got to hear and watch this from far away. He lived in São

Paulo, Brazil and I lived in Utah, United States. He passed away in April of 2020. My relationship with him was as good as it could be before he got ill and I kind of prepared my heart/ mind for the inevitable that was coming sometime in a near future.

Then there was my mother. She had been ill with a heart condition for years. She came to the States for a diagnose. The doctor said she needed open heart surgery to fix a valve. She opted for no surgery. The whole family was up in arms and wanted her to have the surgery. I supported her in her decision. However, it promised declining health for the remainder of her life. The choice was hers to make, and so she did. As time went on, she got progressively worse and she left us in August of 2020. My relationship with her was as good as it could be before she passed.

I was the only child, and my parents passed away a little over three months from each other. I had to go to Brazil to take care of legal matters for both deaths. I got to go through all my mother's things, select what I wanted to keep and give or sell everything else. My dad's wife took care of him during his illness. I am very grateful she was by his side through it all.

Being an only child, reality hit hard when I realized both my parents are gone, within a little over three months from each other. I fell into old patterns. I ate my emotions all the way through. Sad, but that's how I dealt with it. And, being in Brazil after thirteen years, I had to have the delicious things that I can't get here :)

Do I miss them? YES! Do I love them? Of course! Do I know they are in a better place with no more health issues, no more pain, no more suffering? Absolutely! Do I know they would like me to live my life to the best I can and they are watching over me? No doubt! Do I get sad at times? Shed a tear and long to talk to them? Indeed! Inevitable! I have felt their presence very close and I have felt their love. It gives me comfort.

I can't change what happened. I can and I am creating room, adapting and growing for/from their departure. When it hurts, I take it to God and He gives me comfort and peace. Grief comes in different forms from relationships, death, loss of job, loss of health, you name it, it knocks the wind out of our sails and we get to be in that moment, alone.

How do we deal with that? Relationships are complicated at times. It takes two to tangle or mangle it. Sometimes they get interrupted and there is not a thing we can do about it. We grieve the loss of it. We sometimes are at a loss because of it, and we must learn to live with the new reality. Because it is not in our power to make it better. So we grieve. Some of us get to grieve through the loss of jobs, health, emotional disaster. I beg you to please take a hold of grief, don't let it take a hold of you. What do I mean? Grief is hard and powerful. But you are in charge of your heart and mind. The loss of whatever/whomever you are grieving is majestic, I get that. Your heart and mind are in your control. Take charge - make room for it, don't give your soul to it. You are still alive! Grieving as you may be, time still moving, your heart is still beating and reality is still coming to you each day you wake up.

I look at the memories, the moments of life and love that were created because they were a part of my existence and I was of theirs. The relationships that were cut off or are on hold because of circumstances beyond my control are a reason to mourn, not a reason to live in sadness, negativity or hurt.

MOURN: to be sorrowful; to express grief or sorrow; to grieve.

To mourn constantly impedes us from loving with our whole heart, from finding joy, from being present and enjoying the journey, from freedom of the soul. Consider this: We are miracles who grow each day. We are blessed with love in our lives, blessed with people we love and love us. When we get separated for whatever reason; we should be grateful for all that we had as we have it.

The times I have grieved, I have let it go deep into my soul, I've been broken by it, I've given myself into it. It was all consuming. I had to learn to take charge, to make room for it. It has changed me in ways for which I am so very grateful! I used to be too soft, too worried about things that didn't matter so much, and I now, don't give my soul as before. If you let it, toughness comes from being broken beyond repair. Grieve as you need to, we all do. Do it how it works for you. It is no one else's business. Take your time. Yet, please take a step every day in the direction to where you are meant to be headed. With love for self and for whomever you are grieving, take a deep breath and find the joy in the experience. It is there, you just need to look for it.

SMALL CHECK UP

1. Is grief controlling me?
2. Am I looking for/remembering the good in what I had?
3. Am I allowing God to help me?
4. Is grief helping me grow? If not, how can it?
5. Am I putting my pieces back together?
6. Is grief taking a lot of time out of my present life? With my loved ones?
7. What can I do to make grief a part of life, not life itself?

14. LOVE

To be in love…before we can love anyone else, we must love ourselves. We can't give what we don't have, we can't share what we don't know and we can't feel loved when we don't love ourselves. We must recognize it to participate in it.

LOVE: An affection of the mind excited by the beauty and worth of any kind; or by the qualities of an object which communicate pleasure, sensual or intellectual. It is the opposite of hatred.

It was hard to love all of me. There are too many pages in my book of life that I don't read out loud. But I finally learned and understood that all I've been through has made me who I am today. All of the bad and the ugly things have brought me here. I can't help it, but have compassion for those pages that I don't read out loud.

We believe love comes from the heart. And it does. However, the mind has to be in coherence with it (coherence - connection). We create emotions in our minds, so, we must have a willing mind to LOVE :) If our collection of experiences tell us it is not safe to be vulnerable with ourselves or others, then, as you may, it won't work. We all are lovable. YES, WE ARE!

We all were born with light and unconditional love within ourselves. Environment and people influenced us in such way that we may develop fear of love/being loved and shining our light.

OR...

Environment and people influenced us in such way that we are encouraged to shine our light as bright as it goes and to love and be loved unconditionally and completely. And of course, everything in between.

My father was survivor of the Korean War. He was from North Korea. Oriental people (from my perspective) are reserved observers and don't show much emotion. It was understood my father loved me. There was no need to show it with hugs and kisses or words of affirmation.

I am a hugger and love to show and speak affection. That didn't work well with him. I remember the first time he came to visit me in the States with his wife, I was a new mom and he got to see his first grandchild, my daughter. I gave him a hug, he stood there with his arms down, not knowing what to do. I told him, "Dad, hug me back." It was a different experience for him.

My mother was affectionate and we spoke that language freely. My nature is to love deeply, I got hurt many times because of it. I've learned to be reserved, and not to so readily trust. Which is sad, but as I've experienced, the reality of many.

Love is kind, gentle, generous, non judgmental, caring, desirable, happy, present, dependable, respectful, trusting and trust worthy.

What love is NOT: is selfish, unkind, insecure, jealous, brutal, judgmental, disempowering, vengeful, miserable, absent, flighty, disrespectful, not trusting and not trust worthy.

Some people love because that's all they know. Some people can't love, because they never have been loved and haven't put the effort into it. Love can be scary (unknown) and exciting (happy) at the same time. Remember to check if the person cares, respects and is worthy of your heart before you give it to them! HA! You can try :)

Love and light make the world go around. The more people who love, the better the world works. The more empowered people we encounter, the more empowered we become. Love and light are essential to life. Open hearts and minds help us to welcome and embrace love and light.

Children are grand examples of love. They love unconditionally, all the time and forgive quickly, no judgment. Judgment is a learned behavior, not a birthright. Consider how much happier, easier and brighter life would be if we did it too!

As adults, we sometimes get offended or hurt and hold on to it very tight for a very long time. How does that serve you and those around you?

It doesn't. Resentment starts rotting inside the minute it is born.

Love is as powerful as we let it be. Unfortunately, we tend to choose the other stuff that impedes love from taking root, growing and flourishing. Keep in mind, loving without conditions keeps us in light. Light shining brightly keeps us loving and lovable. Being loving and lovable touches hearts and creates hope. Hope keeps us shinning and loving.

Love is so powerful! If we only knew, believed and acted accordingly! It heals, forgives, empowers and encourages the action of loving back. The love of Christ is perfect love; it is there for us to partake and to share. Be kind to yourself and others. Love will help you do that.

SMALL CHECK UP

1. Am I loving in my thoughts and speech?
2. Am I kind to myself? Do I love and accept every part of me?
3. How can I be kinder in thought and deed?

4. Am I insecure in relationships? Why?

5. Am I judgmental of self and people?

6. How can I be kinder?

7. Do I love without expectations? Am I all in?

15. COMFORT ZONES

Comfort zones are comfortable; they are also the place of no growth, change, challenge and absolutely no soul development. Comfort zones are the place we are the same yesterday, today and forever. It is safe because there is no risk. We are familiar with the process. We do what is expected and obtain the same result - EVERY SINGLE TIME. In the comfort zone we can have expectations that are safe.

What do I mean? We KNOW if we act in a certain way, we will produce a certain result. If we dare not to challenge ourselves, we will never change. Change should be a constant in life!

Ourselves included! When we learn something good or great, we should apply it to life itself. What will happen? Who knows?

Meeting new people and building relationships! Sounds scary? It shouldn't. There are no accidents in whom we meet, love and care for.

"In friendship... we think we have chosen our peers. In reality a few years difference in the dates of our births, a few more miles between certain houses, the choice of one university instead of another...
the accident of a topic being raised at a first meeting — any of these chances might have kept us apart. But for a Christian, there are, strictly speaking no chances. A secret master of ceremonies has been at work. Christ, who said to the disciples, "Ye have not chosen me, but I have chosen you," can truly say to every group of Christian friends, "Ye have not chosen one another but I have chosen you for one another." The friendship is not a reward for our

discriminating and good taste in finding one another out. It is the instrument by which God reveals to each of us the beauty of others."

—C. S. Lewis - The Four Loves

Comfort zones are killers of dreams. We either be comfortable or build a beautiful life. The comfort zone is a place where we enjoy no risks, no failure (which is really packed with insights and good lessons), no success, no thrill.

In being comfortable, we experience no growth. We never go places if we never leave! By leaving what is familiar and comfortable, we get to gain courage to face the storms, faith to get us through them, joy in success, wisdom in failure, understanding in experience, excitement in dream building, love in opening our hearts and entering into relationships... Being uncomfortable is challenging at times, but it is wonderful and empowering all the time.

Here are some situations that most of us choose comfort zone without knowing:

- Staying put and not applying for that harder job because it is no use.

- Scratching that big dream because it has never been done, it is impossible and you don't know where to start.

- Eating the same foods, other people will cook differently and you may not like it.

- Staying in the same city because it is familiar and you know it well.

- Doing what your family has always done. It is not in the cards to go to college or heaven forbid, to start a business.

- Believing society and your place in it.

- Can't change your income bracket, housing and social circle.

- Can't change your health, fitness and attitude. It is in my genes to be fat.

- Can't develop a new talent.

- Not expanding your mind by traveling, reading good books, learning a new culture.

- Not getting a second opinion of a diagnosis from a doctor.
- Not becoming the expert on something you are passionate about by not educating yourself about it.

These are few, but it gives you some ideas. And all of these can be changed! We learn daily, if interested. Education is not only found in schools, it is found in books, people and everyday life. Dare to share what you know. Seek to learn what you don't!

We are made to dream. Dreaming keeps us going/growing/becoming. To give up on a dream is to give up on a great life. Dream realizers are the people who change the world, change how they live and change who they are for the better and get closer to their potential. Dreaming with God is the same as entering a miracle factory and running the place for our profit. Pleasures come in many ways.

Food is an experience! How it looks, smells, taste and the health benefits! I always say, "I can try anything once." I am glad to report that there are very few dishes I wouldn't eat again. Broaden your horizons! It can be fun - keep an open mind :)

I love traveling and not by choice; I've moved more than I would like. In those moves, I've met wonderful people, learned of different cultures, enjoyed amazing unfamiliar foods, attended different social events and I am a better person for it.

Thank heavens, science has proven we can change DNA. So whatever it is that your family has been stuck on for generations, it is your job to get un-stuck. Go to college, if that is your desire. Stop drinking, if you are aware you need to stop. Eat healthier and get fit if you think you should. The change can and should start somewhere - why not with you?

Society fluctuates. Some go up and some go down: your assigned place is not permanent. It depends on you. Where you live, what you drive, where you work… It is all personal choice. It takes time, but it is possible to change where you are in society.

Our bodies are amazing! The mind is the most powerful 'computer' in existence. When we focus on, we can change even our DNA, generational issues and emotional history. We are empowered to health when we take control of ourselves with our minds and hearts :) How about a new talent? Sometimes we think, "There is no way in Hades that I can do that!" Or, "I would love to, but I don't know how." Explore it and learn how!

For example:

I didn't know I could speak another language until the need and desire arose and I went for it.

Today, I enjoy cooking and have been told time and time again that the food that I cook tastes great. I didn't know how to cook, but always looked for yummy recipes and added my own twist to it to make it better.

I didn't know how to sew, but had a friend who is an artist seamstress. She taught me how to sew and I can hold my own in sewing.

I don't have an artistic bone in my body, but I do enjoy simple water coloring.

I didn't know I could write a book until I started putting the pen to the paper and enjoying as the words kept on writing themselves.

Talents are awaiting for you to start developing them... outside the comfort zone. Ready? Set...GO!

SMALL CHECK UP

1. Am I uncomfortable or too comfortable every day?
2. Am I experiencing growth regularly?
3. When was the last time I felt challenged and excited about life?
4. Do I have any old beliefs that are holding me back?
5. Am I learning something new?
6. Am I realizing a dream? Do I have a dream?
7. What am I passionate about?

16. BLAME, NOT A GOOD THING

When was the last time you blamed yourself or someone?

BLAME: to censure, to assign responsibility for a fault for 'hurt' or 'injury.'

"Someone is to blame."

Usually when something bad happens, the blame belongs somewhere. This phrase would be used way less if:

- We acted more instead of reacting.
- We listened to understand instead of to respond.
- We thought before we spoke harshly.
- We would observe instead of judge.

- We would do things out of love instead of expectation of reciprocation.

Why do we look for/give blame for unfortunate events? Think on that for a minute. Really, bad things happen, someone or something somewhere and sometime started it the chain of events. Why do we feel necessary to make it someone's fault? So we can be right? Innocent? Victorious? Powerful? On the right side of the fight? For what?

- There is no prize that comes with blame.
- There is no podium to stand on.
- There is no medal or trophy to be awarded.

Blaming self or someone only makes it so the one being blamed feels ashamed.

ASHAMED : affected by shame; confused by a consciousness of guilt or inferiority; by failure or disappointment.

Why do we do it? It doesn't feel good. It doesn't help. It doesn't do any good! So, instead of blaming, why don't we let go?

Instead of blaming someone for personal unhappiness, let's take responsibility and create our own happiness, wherever we are, however life looks! Look for the ways we can be happy and go for it. NO ONE besides ourselves knows what that is!

Instead of blaming for poor performance or low results, how about looking for what can be improved and get behind that to change results? Or how about blaming someone for losing a thing? When I lose something, it is because I no longer need it. It was sad to lose my silver ring with the moon and star, but someone else needed more than I did. I blamed myself for a minute, then let go and wished well to its new owner.

IT TAKES A LOT OF ENERGY TO
EXERCISE BLAME AND TO RECEIVE IT.

LET GO OF THE NEED TO BLAME
AND OF THE NEED TO ACCEPT THE
BLAME AND GUILT.

LIFE IS MUCH GREATER THAT WAY! :)

SMALL CHECK UP

1. Do I feel the need to blame myself or others? Why?

2. Do I take the blame so others won't have to?

3. Do I blame others so I can feel better about myself?

4. Am I in charge of my own happiness or do I expect others to make me happy?

5. How much energy am I spending on looking for who to blame?

6. Do I accept blame when given?

7. Do I know how to take no shame when being blamed by someone else? Do I let go?

17. FORGIVENESS IS NECESSARY

Forgiveness does not get to be conditional, explained or purchased. Forgiveness is complete, simple enough and given freely.

Sometimes forgiving self is the hardest to do. The process of repentance is the sweetest or it can be bitter if we choose. We make mistakes daily. Some days are better than others, and some are worse than most.

"Resentment is like drinking poison and then hoping it will kill your enemies."

—Nelson Mandela

Have you known people who are so bitter because of the resentment they insist on caring throughout their lives? They are quick to judge, blame and be the victim? They have chosen to drink poison several times and the poison corroded their souls, deemed their light and lowered their vibration.

How about people who don't repent? Or those who have hurt us deeply and either are not aware or simply don't care?

Forgiveness is the vitamin for the soul of the individual exercising it. To forgive is to truly let go of whatever it is that hurt you, offended or made you angry. Do you want to know a secret? Nobody can hurt you, offend you or "make" you angry. Those are choices. We chose to be hurt by someone (who is probably hurting themselves, which is why they said/did what they said/did), we choose to be offended and we choose the emotion with which we react.

- PLEASE CONSIDER TAKING ACTION INSTEAD.

Words are powerful and most people don't put much thought into the words they are saying. They speak without considering the effect it may have on someone else. Before getting offended, take a look at the person that is "offending" you. Look at where they've been and where they are. That helps a lot.

How about people who rob and steal from you? (individuals or businesses) Every THING is God's... period. We get to be stewards over all with which we are blessed with. When we die, it stays behind. The Lord gives us things to be stewards over it. When someone is dishonest and steals from us, what we do with the experience is what matters.

Divine abundance is infinite. There is more where that came from. Do we get stuck on holding resentment, or sometimes hatred, or do we learn the lesson and go on creating more abundance for ourselves and others?

How about abusive parents? There are those out there who come inches from destroying their children's souls, or sometimes succeed in doing so. And they will have to answer to God for that one. But as an abused child, we are much better off to forgive and change the traditions of the fathers. Break the cycle! Change behavior!

Forgive so you are free. Forgive so you can change it for the better for your children and posterity. Forgive so you can be a better human.

What about crimes that are heinous and change your life forever? I've worked for a public defender/criminal law lawyer, I had to put files together so he could create a defense case for crimes which didn't happen to me and I had a hard time with it. There are people out there who do pure evil.

However, I live in a country which has a form of government that is good. We have a Constitution and one of the things in that inspired document is that everyone has the right to a fair trial. You break men's laws, you get to be tried by men's court. However, there are higher laws broken when men's laws are broken; and that is where

I can work on forgiveness. That job with the lawyer broke my heart in so many levels! But!!!! I've learned to pray for the victims, to send them light and love and to pray for the criminals, so they will hopefully realize what they did and start on the repentance process.

We do what we do because we know what we know. We are constantly learning we are who we are because of what we've experienced. We change when we do because we chose to create a better life for ourselves and those whom we influence on the path of our journey.

When one chooses to be offended or hurt, the antidote is to forgive and move on. When we choose to feel devastated for the loss of money or things, forgiveness brightens up the day.

How about the ungrateful? Yes, those whom we serve and to whom we give things and not one ounce of gratitude is returned? Gratitude is a divine virtue. As parents, kids can be very ungrateful; it is part of the program. They learn that virtue as they get older (become adults) and even then, sometimes it is not shown.

It is not your job to make life miserable in hopes they learn it sooner than later. It is your job to live by example and forgive them for their selfishness and complete oblivious attitude.

Forgive them as you would like to be forgiven of your graver wrong doings. In a nutshell, only forgive as much as you would like to be forgiven and as often as you need forgiving.

SMALL CHECK UP

1. Do I need to forgive myself? Am I letting go of my wrong doings, learning the lesson from it and doing better from now on?
2. Am I bitter for holding grudges?
3. Who do I need to forgive?
4. Am I at peace in my heart?
5. Do I take things personally? Should I just let go?
6. Do I have an ownership problem? Do I understand that I am a steward of the possessions God blessed me with for me to enjoy and share?
7. Do I forgive as much as I want to be forgiven and as often as I need to be forgiven?

18. JUDGING

Judging sucks! Being judged, even more! When I was seventeen, I moved to Utah from Sao Paulo, Brazil. My mom and I lived with my aunt (her sister) and family. My aunt pointed out a certain man and told my mom she wished he would marry me, she thought it would be a good match. My mother said, "Good luck, he is too handsome, he will never look at my daughter."

I was devastated by that judgment of my mother! However, two years later we met, and seven months after we met, we got married.

Humans tend to judge, either out of insecurity or jealousy. It does no one any good.

JUDGING: to form an opinion or conclusion about someone or something.

This chapter is a short one. Only judge as hard as you would like to be judged. We don't know where people have been, how they got there or how long they've been there. They don't know where we've been, how we traveled and what we've lived through. So, DON'T JUDGE, PERIOD.

If you are being judged, don't give it room in your heart or mind. God is mindful and He's got you. Focus on light, love and high vibration emotions.

BE DEAF TO THE CRITICS BE BLIND TO THE ENVY OR INSECURITIES. BE KIND TO THEM ALL. MOST IMPORTANTLY ONLY JUDGE AS HARD AS YOU WANT TO BE JUDGED BY GOD.

SMALL CHECK UP

1. Am I judging people for their behavior/speech/thought?

2. Am I offended by the critics? Why?

3. Is people's judgments of me keeping me from doing what I know is right for me?

4. Am I allowing judgments to offend me?

5. Am I paying too much attention to other's lives and neglecting my own?

6. Am I exercising compassion?

7. Do I feel peace in my thoughts?

19. ENJOY THE JOURNEY

Have you heard people say "Life is full of ups and downs"? It doesn't have to be. If you believe or expect to have many ups and downs, you will accomplish exactly that: a rollercoaster ride.

Have you consider another way to travel your journey? We can keep on going up! As we achieve goals, enjoy the place we arrive for a while… until we outgrow it and then go up again with new goals, repeat!

Life is about focus. Remember the law of time? We can't rewind, change or stop it.

There is a the law of polarity. If something awful happened, it is our job alone to look for the something wonderful that is in it as well.

I used to be a day planner queen back in the day. By that I mean if it wasn't written down, it didn't get done. Until one day my 5 year old was singing with the Alabama CD I was playing in the car:

"I'm in a hurry to get things done.
Oh, I rush and rush until life's not fun.
All I really gotta do is live and die.
Even I'm in a hurry and don't know why."
Alabama - I'm in a Hurry
(And Don't Know Why)

Then in all her kindergarten wisdom she said, " That is you, Mom. You are always in a hurry and life is no fun."

Wow? That hit me hard! The day planner went away and I did more "un-scheduled"things. I was rigid in all things. Being a literal person, that is not a very good combination. You guessed it…I had huge ups and downs.

It has been a journey! I am learning all the time and everywhere I've been. There are days that are so gray that it is hard to look for the bright side in it. But it is there to be found.

So, take a break and look around. Look for what makes the day better. Find ways to enjoy the journey, but make sure to fill your own cup before you serve the crowd. Align yourself with God, so when you do His work, you trust the outcome, even when you can't see it. Sad things happen in life. What we do with it is what matters. Living in the present free of fear because we trust the outcome (God is all over it) is a very big step in changing the mind set.

God is generous in His blessings. Call upon the ones you are ready to receive . Don't name them, just call on the ones that are ready for you. You are stronger than you think, stick to it. Stop fighting and ride the wave. It will take you to shore.

Keep in mind: re-acting usually makes things worse, ACTING shifts things your way. Everyone has good in them. It is not as obvious in some people as in others. But, it is there :) Money can be tight or non-existent. Look for better ways to produce/receive/accept/enjoy money. Money is not evil.

People come and go. Some show up out of thin air, some stay a while and are gone for good, some are there forever and some keep on popping up. Enjoy their presence in the present.

There might not be a repeat. Life is too short to let resentment change your vibration. Life is too precious to allow judgment to keep you from loving/being loved.

We find what we look for, look for good things. Enjoy them when you find it and put your goodness into the day you are creating. We exchange energy as we are all interconnected on a journey going home. We do so at different speeds, in different modes of transportation, and are on different paths. Yet, we are all children of the same God, recipients of His love and mercy. Each of us are on a path with different geography, topography and altitude. Let our focus and attitude make it the best journey yet!

My journey has been full and very challenging at times. However, wherever I've been, I found good people/things/events. I can see that my attitude towards whatever I've been through has made it enjoyable or miserable. I've felt alone at times, even in a crowd. I've felt peace in the middle of the storm and I've created joy.

There are blessings, miracles and angels (pre-mortal, mortal and immortal) everywhere to help us on our journey. I choose to be an instrument in God's hands every day. My morning prayer is to let Him know I am here and ready to be used by Him. That has helped me to be able to show up for people out of nowhere, in an answer to their prayers. I've had many people do the same for me. And, I have had the sweet experience of receiving help from the spiritual realm.

What a wonderful thing to be in a place where all of that can happen, be felt and enjoyed! Take time to look for it all. Find what you are looking for and in that finding, your life becomes joyous to be lived. Enjoy the journey; it was created with you in mind!

SMALL CHECK UP

1. Am I taking time to enjoy the day as the miracle that it is, because I know it won't be repeated?

2. Am I in too much of a hurry? Should I slow down?

3. Am I too busy to do the things that are really important to me?

4. Is my time being spent in things that bring me joy?

5. When was the last time I realized a dream of mine?

6. Does my life make me smile?

7. Do I love and allow myself to be loved?

20. NOTES FROM JOURNEY TO WHOLENESS

Here is a review of the checklist on using this book:

WORDS ARE POWERFUL

Think before you speak, speak your truths with kindness and be positive in your words. Start with the words you think/speak to about yourself.

Questions to ask:

- Why am I thinking/saying this?
- If negative/"constructive" criticism, how can I change it?
- When addressing someone, ask yourself, would I like to be spoken to this way?
- How can I kindly speak my truths?
- Am I changing my thoughts to better ones?

TAKE ACTION INSTEAD OF REACTING

We always have a choice to ACT or REACT. When things get hot, we usually go into react mode. It is easy to get into, self preservation/defense and "let's make them feel as bad as they are making me feel"… or … the most common, "I am RIGHT".

Take your power back! STOP and think before you reply. Sometimes the reply is silence.

Questions to ask:

- AM I acting or reacting?
- Does this needs to be addressed?
- How can I take action to better the situation?
- What is important here? How can I make it understandable with kindness?
- Am I cool headed enough to address this? If not, explain and walk away.

THERE IS ALWAYS A CHOICE

Life is made of choices. We make choices every day. From getting out of bed, to what we eat, what emotions we feed, choosing forgiveness/revenge, service, looking for the good in people/events/places, wasting time, living in the present, bettering ourselves, and letting go of hurt.

Questions to ask:

- Is my choice in this matter the best one for all involved, self included?
- Am I choosing out of fear?
- Is my choice educated and made from the heart?
- Is this choice going to bring good results?
- Is this my choice or my peers'?

LAWS

The laws of God are unbreakable and unchangeable. We can break ourselves against it or we can obey the laws and obtain great results in our endeavors. The laws of men are breakable and changeable. It would serve us best to find the law of God that we need to observe to achieve our goals.

Questions to ask:

- What law covers this issue?
- Am I aware of what I need to do?
- How can I obey that law better?
- How am I changing my thinking/behavior/ speaking to abide by that law?
- Am I prayerful about it?

FEAR

Fear is the natural human reaction to the unknown, the dreadful things, and the hurt and all the people/events/places that pose some sort of doubt or threat. We control how intense/ paralyzing/inexistent it can be. Fear grows with doubts and dies with faith.

Questions to ask:

- Why am I afraid? (Go as far as you can, it really makes the reason less powerful)
- What am I doubting that can be done/ created/spoken?
- What emotions of light can I focus on to change the fear into hope?

- Am I giving my fears to God?
- Am I trusting God is helping me?

EMOTIONS ARE POWERFUL

Emotions are powerful movers and shakers of people. The more passionate we are about something, the faster we get to it. The more negative, unbelieving we are about it, the further we push it away. We are made of what we feel and we feel what we believe we are.

Questions to ask:

- Am I in my purpose in this choice?
- Are my emotions in check?
- Am I being positive, loving and patient with self/ others?
- Am I living a joyous meaningful life?
- Am I acting from a place of peace or reacting from a place of hurt?
- Am I being open minded?

WE ALL MAKE MISTAKES, GET OVER IT

Mistakes can be costly, painful and life changing. The good thing is, we ALL make mistakes; today or tomorrow, we shall do something we wish we didn't. Take the lesson (s) mistakes bring and be better for it. Let go of the guilt, grow from it and be better for it.

Questions to ask:

- How can I make this better?
- What would I do differently to avoid this outcome?
- Am I holding on to guilt?
- What did I learn from this?
- What were the warnings so I can avoid it next time?

SCHOOL OF HARD KNOCKS

Learning from experience and growing from it. When we learn by trial and error, it seems to me that the lesson sticks better and deeper. So, this thing we call life is really the place and time we learn what is necessary to become our potential. Hopefully, we are letting go of the need to be bitter about hard stuff and choose to be better because we made it through.

Questions to ask:

- How can I get through this and find things to enjoy today?
- I know I can deal with this, it is here, which way is the best way for me?
- What is the lesson?
- How can I keep one foot in front of the other? What do I need to do in my next step?
- How can I love and serve through this?

FOCUS, IT IS IMPORTANT

On what we focus is what/where we accomplish/create/ arrive. If we focus on fear, we literally will create what we fear. If we focus on good/positive/light/high vibration, we shall be surrounded of good things/people/events.

Questions to ask:

- Is my focus light/positive?
- What can I change to make it better?
- Am I focusing on the result I desire so the way to it can present itself?

- Do I focus on doing good to myself and others?
- Do I need to change focus? (DAILY QUESTION)

BOUNDARIES ARE HEALTHY

Boundaries are healthy. Walls are not. What's the difference? Boundaries are build on respect for self and others. Walls are built to keep people far and away. Healthy boundaries create healthy relationships.

Questions to ask:

- Did I give this person power over how I feel about myself?
- Is this a healthy relationship? Do we respect each other, are we kind?
- Do I need to say no?
- Do I need to leave?
- Am I standing for my truths

PERSPECTIVE

We are all individuals with unique individuality. No two are the same. Siblings are raised by the same parents, but because of their individuality and perspective of life, they are unique and original. My perspective is right for me as yours is right for you.

Questions to ask:

- Are there other perspectives I need to be considering?
- Is my perspective educated and broad? - Is my perspective in need of more information?
- What are my family's perspectives? Are they valid? Do I need to separate myself from it?
- Am I listening to understand or to react?

BE A MAGNET OF GOOD THINGS

To attract good, we must be focusing on good ourselves. Honor the shift. Let people leave. Leave yourself, if necessary and welcome the new crowd that shows up. As we leave the comfort zone, the scenery changes, the empowerment increases and the vibration goes up. We attract and are attracted to people, events, and places alike. Enjoy the journey.

Questions to ask:

- Am I in a positive/empowering circle/place?
- Am I generating good energy, light and vibes?
- Are my dreams/goals greater than who I am today? Am I changing to achieve them?
- Who and what am I attracting?
- Who and what is attracting me?

GRIEF, IT HURTS

Do it how you need to, for however long you need to and let God comfort you. The loss is great, the sorrow immeasurable and it seems like it will never end. Please consider the power you have over your heart and mind. Choose to feel joy, a little at a time, a step at a time; just start walking. Give thanks for the portion of life you were able to enjoy for whatever or whomever you are grieving and let God heal your broken heart.

Questions to ask:

- What is one joy I can remember from this sorrow? Give thanks for it.
- Have I allowed God to heal me? Have I asked?

- How can I start putting one foot in front of the other?
- Can I give thanks for this person/event/place?
- How can I comfort those around me?

LOVE

Love is powerful and empowering. To love and be loved, one must love themselves. Love forgives and lets it go. It builds up people and empowers them. Love is a verb and a noun. To love is to understand and compromise, to give without expectation, to speak their love language, and is service, receiving, supporting. Love is beautiful and it beautifies all that it touches.

Questions to ask:

- Can I honestly say I love myself? (all of me)
- Am I loving unconditionally?
- Does love bring me joy?
- Do I feel the love of God for me?
- Am I afraid of love? (if yes, keep asking why, until you find the answer)

COMFORT ZONES

Comfort zones are awesome!!! No risk, no challenge, no failure. There is also no growth, no success, no achievement, no change. You do what you always did and get what you always got. You never get anywhere if you don't go beyond the comfort zone.

Questions to ask:

- How can I challenge myself today to be better than yesterday?
- What can I learn today?
- What can I do to accomplish my goals/ dreams?
- What can I do in my relationships/work/ life that will improve them?
- What do I know that I can share and help someone?

BLAME, NOT A GOOD THING

Blame is easy to do and take, It must be someone's fault. We mostly blame when things go wrong. Very few times you will see someone blaming success on someone else; most likely they will want the credit for it. Consider how much better it would be if we fix the wrong, better the project, pay attention and help heal the relationship.

Questions to ask:

- How can I improve on this?
- What can be done different?
- Who can/will help me?
- What do I need to learn?
- What did I learn from this?

FORGIVENESS IS NECESSARY

Forgiveness is good for the soul. To forgive frees the forgiver of bitterness, resentment and hurt/offense. It also frees the forgiven of the guilt, shame and sorrow. Forgive always. Even the ones who are not sorry, who are unaware they need to apologize or hurt you with intent.

Questions to ask:

- Do I need to apologize here?
- Do I need to forgive myself?
- Am I holding resentment/ offense towards anyone?

- Am I bitter for something I need to let go?
- Have I let go of the emotions that create this pain/resentment/hurt?

JUDGING

Simply said, judging is hard and we judge. We will be judged by One that matters. Because of insecurities, envy and dislike, we may judge. Our judgment of others will do little or nothing to them, but a lot to ourselves. It carries a lot of weight on the one judging. Only judge as heavily and you want to be judged.

Questions to ask:

- Am I judging anyone?
- What is the good in this person/event/place?
- How can I stop judging?
- What can I learn from this?
- Lord, please help me to stop judging, I need help!

ENJOY THE JOURNEY

Enjoy the journey wherever you are. Look for the good in it, embrace it and share it. The sun will rise tomorrow the rain from the storm will dry and the future will look better when we see how blessed we are and how good we have it.

Question to ask:
- What good thing happened today?
- What good can I see in people I talk with today?
- How is my life better today than yesterday?
- How can I help someone?
- What good habit can I start and keep up for 3 months?

This book was a processing, if you read through it and answer the questions, you've done some work!

EMPOWERING I AM STATEMENTS FOR AFTER YOU DO THE PROCESSING IN THE BOOK:

Words are Powerful

I speak kind words that are empowering to self and others.
My words build and empower those that hear them, myself included.

I speak my truths kindly and listen to understand.
I speak in the way I would like to be spoken to.
I chose wisely the words that come after "I AM."
I am positive, light and vibrating high I speak from my heart.

Take Action Instead of Reacting

I think before I act, "People's opinions of me are none of my business."
I look for different perspectives and make choices accordingly.
I am free to choose, I choose wisely.
I let go of the need to defend myself or to be right.
I let go of anger and chose inner peace.
I am free of the need to react

There is Always a Choice

I always have a choice.
I choose light, I choose love, I choose positivity, I choose high vibration.
I chose to look for the good in people/events/places.
I chose inner peace as the outcome.
I chose to do my best today.
I chose God I chose freedom.

Laws

I am aware of the laws with which I am working.
I work with the laws of God.
My personal laws are congruent with God's laws.
The laws of God are there to help me succeed.
Divine laws work well with my divine nature.
I am grateful for God's laws.
I feel God's love in His laws.

Fear

I am courageous, because I am full of faith.
Fear is powerless over me.
I trust the outcome is divinely planned for me.
Fear is a thing of the past.
I am fearless, I give fear to God every time it shows up.
I embrace faith, fear goes away.
God is with me, nothing prevails against me.

Emotions Are Powerful

I choose emotions of high frequency.
I give negative emotions to God and let it be.
I rule my emotions.
Positive emotions help me grow.

I feed my passion high vibration emotions.
I spread good emotions wherever I am.
I believe in love, I am love, I love, I am loved.

We All Make Mistakes, Get Over It

I am doing my best with what I know right now.
I forgive myself for poor choices in the past.
I am who I am today because of the lessons I've learned.
A mistake made is a lesson learned I make choices daily, I am choosing wisely.
Perfection is fully developed, complete, finished, flawlessness is an illusion.
I regress when I resent, I progress when I forgive.
I am letting resentment go every day of my life.

School of Hard Knocks

I learn as I go about my day.
I am better for the things I have overcome.
I take time to enjoy the day I am enjoying the journey.
I love myself as I am.
I and doing my best with what I know.
I am free to think, speak and choose.

Focus, It is Important

I am focusing on good things with empowering emotions.

I am realizing my dreams, my focus is on creating them, fear and doubts are gone.

I am a positive, light high vibrating soul.

Live is beautiful; every storm runs out of rain.

I am strong, able and full of faith, all things are possible.

Everything works out for my greatest and highest good.

I let go of the need to need to know the outcome.

Boundaries Are Healthy

I am safe I respect and honor my boundaries and that of others .

I can and do say "NO" when necessary.

I create healthy boundaries.

I tear down walls and replace them with boundaries.

I connect with people in a healthy way.

I enforce my boundaries.

Perspective

Different ways to look at things expand my vision.

I am open to new insights.

I am aware of different perspectives.
We are all unique, and we see life differently, it is great to be different.
I look at things from different angles, with an open mind.
I grow as I see things from different perspectives.
I chose to do things the best way from where I am.

Be a Magnet of Good Things

I am positive, light and vibrating high.
I attract what I send out, sending out the best I have.
I am empowered by God, which attracts miracles into my life.
I am what I believe, I attract what I am.
I speak the things I desire, I AM____.
I let go of the negative in my life, I choose to stay positive, I attract positive.
I am abundant of all good things.

Grief, It Hurts

I am letting go of the sadness in my heart.
I am looking for joy I am grateful for peace in my life, I am creating a happier day today.

I am giving the grief to God, He comforts me.
My heart is getting stronger, I feel love.
I choose to remember the happiness and good memories from this sorrow.
I am lighter, today is a better day.

Love

I love myself, every part of me.
I love unconditionally.
I love without expectations.
I love deeply.
I am lovable.
I am empowered by the love of God.
I attract love into my life.

Comfort Zones

I am on an adventure and am enjoying life as it comes!
I am growing, learning and loving it.
I chose to leave the comfort zone, I am free to choose.
I am doing different things to obtain different results.
I am taking action from the lessons.

I've learned that I am strong, insightful and smart; I've got this.

I am glad the outcome is unknown, I like it that way

Blame, Not a Good Thing

I take responsibility for my choices and actions.

I let go of the need to blame someone else or myself.

Outcomes are results of the process, we are all part of the process.

I let go of the need to judge who to blame.

I blame no one.

I am at peace with the outcome.

I did my best and that is enough.

Forgiveness is Necessary

I forgive myself, I let go of guilt.

I forgive unconditionally and completely, I change my behavior.

I apologize when necessary and change my behavior.

I am forgiven I forgive and let go completely.

I let go of the hurt and resentment towards self/ people.

I feel God's love as I repent of my doings.

Judging

I let go of the need to judge.
I observe and I learn from the mistakes of others and my own.
I am in charge of my heart, it is judgment free.
I disregard the judgments of others towards me.
I travel light, judgment is heavy, I leave it behind.
I chose where my energy goes;, judgment is a waste of good energy.
Judging hinders progress, I like forward movement.

Enjoy the Journey, It Was Created By You

I am taking time to find joy in each day.
I am creating life, adding joy to it I actively look for joy in every trial.
Joy is an inside job, I work on it daily.
I am creating joyous moments to have joyous memories.
Joy is powerful, it changes my soul.
Joy is part of the divine in me.

21. ON A PERSONAL NOTE:

These are a few things I've learned on my journey to wholeness. I don't claim being perfect at these things, but I know that when I do them, it is very helpful. By sharing them, I went through processing again on issues I thought I had worked through many times!

We are made of layers, in them we progress in healing, thinking and being. Please understand you are powerful! Your mind and heart create what you focus on; health, joy, wealth, dreams, the list goes on. Give it your best shot! Over and over again until you can see your creation! See you in the doing of things!

ACKNOWLEDGMENTS

I am grateful for the help in editing I received from Rhonda Chatterly and Craig Gale, and for the incredible guidance and expertise of Jenn Foster from Elite Online Publishing, without her, I would still be doing research on how to put this book out there.

ABOUT THE AUTHOR

Sarah Moon is an avid student of healing, self-improvement, and perspectives. She has worked with many clients in releasing emotions, energy alignment, and raising vibration. Sarah is passionate about the betterment of life. She is originally from Brazil and moving to Utah at age seventeen has been a life changer.

She is a speaker and loves sharing what she has learned. Her motto is "I'm attached to nothing and open to what life brings."

Sarah is a mother to four amazing kids and the nana to three adorable grandkids. She loves to connect to nature, write, and travel.

Sarah has transformed herself by applying what she has learned over the years, and she has come long way from where she started on her healing journey when at the age of twenty-five she hit suicidal depression.

Sarah is a certified Reiki practitioner and loves aligning people's energy/chakras, releasing emotions, and raising the vibration of individuals, and dwelling places.

Sarah has owned a coaching business for a little over twenty years, she works with clients, speaks, and shares what she has learned.

Visit totalityworkshop.com for more information.